Storm Chasers

by Alice Cary

illustrated by
Rudy Gutierrez

Scott Foresman

Editorial Offices: Glenview, Illinois • New York, New York
Sales Offices: Reading, Massachusetts • Duluth, Georgia
Glenview, Illinois • Carrollton, Texas • Menlo Park, California

A tornado is a strong, wild windstorm. Tornadoes sometimes wail like freight trains. They can do a great deal of damage. They can blow houses down. They can throw cars and vans in the air. They can even sweep trains off their tracks.

Would anyone want to be near storms like these? Yes. Some people do. They are called storm chasers.

When storm chasers glimpse a funnel cloud on the horizon, they are very pleased. They want to learn all they can about tornadoes. They want to learn how and why tornadoes form so that they can help protect people and property. They photograph them. They videotape them. They love these strange storms.

Storm chasing began in the late 1950s. There weren't many pictures of tornadoes then. People did not know much about tornadoes.

A few people wanted to know more. They began to chase strong thunderstorms. Tornadoes begin in these storms.

The first chasers took many pictures. They took notes and began to learn more.

Chasers built tools to help them. One was called TOTO. This small weather machine measured things like wind speed.

Chasers tried to put TOTO where a tornado might land. But it was hard to know the right spot. TOTO was hit only once by a small tornado. Now TOTO is in a museum.

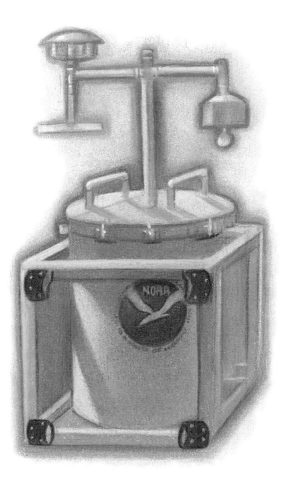

Later scientists sent weather balloons into storms.

In the 1990s scientists started a big tornado project called VORTEX. It used radar and three planes to study tornadoes. The scientists used cars and vans filled with equipment. They raced after the storms. Scientists are still studying the information they got.

One storm chaser named Charles Edwards built a special camera. He called it a "Dillo Cam." When he thinks a tornado will come, he puts the Dillo Cam in the path. He goes to a safe place. But he leaves the video camera behind in the storm.

Finding the right spot to put the Dillo Cam is hard. Edwards was the first person to film the inside of a tornado. His video is very interesting.

Dillo Cam

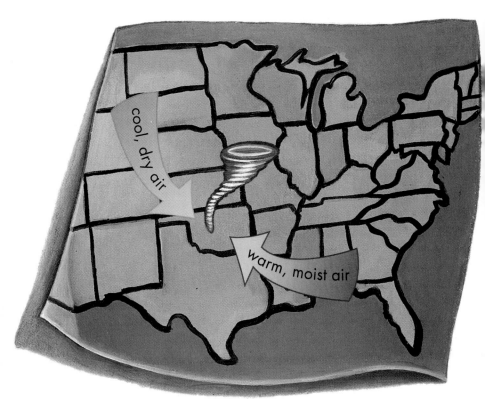

Over the years, chasers have learned a lot about tornadoes. They've learned that tornadoes begin inside big thunderstorms. Warm, moist air meets cool, dry air. The warm air swirls up, faster and faster. If it swirls fast enough, a tornado is born.

The United States has about one thousand tornadoes a year. But the strongest tornadoes—those that destroy whole towns—are rare.

An area of the Midwest has many tornadoes. This area is called "Tornado Alley."

Spring is tornado season. That's when storm chasers head for Tornado Alley.

Who are these chasers? Many are scientists. Some are photographers. Some work for TV stations. Some are students. Some are just people interested in tornadoes. Tornado watching is very dangerous!

How does a chase begin? The National Weather Service predicts when tornadoes may form. But no one knows exactly where, or if, this will happen.

Chasers study weather charts and maps. They decide where to wait. This is called "playing the storm."

Each group drives to a waiting spot. They check the weather with computers, radios, TVs, and phones. Mostly, they watch the sky.

Finding a storm is tricky. Sometimes chasers drive five hundred miles in one day. They may turn around many times. Storm chasing is a big guessing game.

And chasers often make the wrong guess.

Sometimes chasers do spot a tornado.

Up close, a tornado has a wail like a train or plane. Chasers don't want to hear this wail. It means they are too close. No one wants to end up in an accident report! Chasers try to stay a mile or more away from big storms.

Tornadoes can kill. So chasing them is
dangerous. Storm chasers must also be careful of
lightning. Good storm chasers follow many
safety rules.

Chasers report what they see. Their work helps others learn more about tornadoes.

Do you want to learn more about tornadoes? Go to the library. Read books. You may even find magazines for storm chasers. Look for special weather programs on TV. The Internet also has good information about tornadoes.

Maybe one day scientists will know exactly where tornadoes will form.

And maybe scientists will be able to tell how storm chasers can safely follow the wild wind called a tornado.